Taxcafe.co.uk Tax Guides

Master Property Capital Gains Tax
in 2 Hours

How to Calculate it - How to Avoid it

By Carl Bayley BSc ACA
and
Nick Braun PhD

Important Legal Notices:

Taxcafe®
Tax Guide - "Master Property Capital Gains in 2 Hours"

Published by:
Taxcafe UK Limited
67 Milton Road
Kirkcaldy KY1 1TL
Tel: (0044) 01592 560081
Email: team@taxcafe.co.uk

ISBN 1 904608 75 2

First edition, April 2008

Trademarks
Taxcafe® is a registered trademark of Taxcafe UK Limited. All other logos, trademarks, names and logos in this tax guide may be trademarks of their respective owners.

Disclaimer
Before reading or relying on the content of this tax guide please read carefully the disclaimer. If you have any queries then please contact the publisher at team@taxcafe.co.uk.

Disclaimer

1. This guide is intended as general guidance only for individual readers and does NOT constitute accountancy, tax, investment or other professional advice.

2. Neither Taxcafe UK Limited nor the authors can accept any responsibility or liability for loss which may arise from reliance on information contained in this guide.

3. Please note that tax legislation, the law and practices by Government and regulatory authorities (e.g. Revenue & Customs) are constantly changing. We therefore recommend that for accountancy, tax, investment or other professional advice, you consult a suitably qualified accountant, tax specialist, independent financial adviser, or other professional adviser.

4. Please also note that your personal circumstances may vary from the general examples given in this guide and your professional adviser will be able to give specific advice based on your personal circumstances.

5. This guide covers UK taxation only and any references to 'tax' or 'taxation', unless the contrary is expressly stated, refer to UK taxation only. Please note that references to the 'UK' do not include the Channel Islands or the Isle of Man. Foreign tax implications are beyond the scope of this guide.

6. Whilst in an effort to be helpful, this guide may refer to general guidance on matters other than UK taxation, Taxcafe UK Limited does not accept any responsibility or liability for loss which may arise from reliance on such information.

About the Authors & Taxcafe

Carl Bayley is the author of a series of Taxcafe guides designed specifically for the layman. Carl's particular speciality is his ability to take the weird, complex and inexplicable world of taxation and set it out in the kind of clear, straightforward language that taxpayers themselves can understand. As he often says himself, "my job is to translate tax into English".

In addition to being a recognised author, Carl has often spoken on taxation on radio and television, including the BBC's *It's Your Money* programme and the Jeremy Vine Show on Radio 2.

A chartered accountant by training, Carl is also a member of the governing Council of the Institute of Chartered Accountants in England and Wales.

Nick Braun founded Taxcafe.co.uk in 1999, along with his partner, Aileen Smith. As the driving force behind the company, their aim is to provide affordable plain-English tax information for private individuals and investors, business owners, IFAs and accountants.

In the last nine years Taxcafe has become one of the best-known tax publishers in the UK and won several business awards.

Nick has been involved in the tax publishing world since 1989 as a writer, editor and publisher. He holds a doctorate in economics from the University of Glasgow, where he was awarded the prestigious William Glen Scholarship and later became a Research Fellow. Prior to that he graduated with distinction from the University of South Africa, the country's oldest university, earning the highest results in economics in the university's history.

Contents

Chapter 1

Introduction

In October 2007 the Government announced massive changes to capital gains tax.

The new rules apply to all property sales made on or after the 6th of April 2008. It doesn't matter whether you bought your property before or after that date.

For many property investors capital gains tax will now be a lot less complicated and a lot less expensive.

The changes include:

- A flat 18% tax rate
- The scrapping of taper relief, and
- The scrapping of indexation relief.

If you don't know much about taper relief or indexation relief, don't worry. They've now been consigned to the dustbin!

In a further announcement made in January 2008, the Chancellor of the Exchequer also proposed to introduce a new Entrepreneurs Relief for people selling a business. This relief will potentially let you pay just 10% on the first £1 million of your capital gains.

The vast majority of property investors cannot benefit from this relief, however. The only ones that may qualify are owners of furnished holiday lets and certain business owners who sell their trading premises. More on this later.

How Certain Are These Changes?

It's important to stress that, at the time this guide was compiled, the capital gains tax changes were not law yet and probably won't make it onto the actual statute books until July or August 2008.

However, draft legislation containing the changes was published in January and March 2008, making it almost a certainty that the proposals will become law.

Scope of this Guide

The aim of this guide is to give you a thorough grounding in property capital gains tax.

Please note that it does not cover **every** eventuality – that would be impossible in such a short space of time. So please bear in mind the general nature of the information contained here.

To keep life as simple as possible, we're only going to cover the new capital gains tax rules which apply to all property sales taking place from 6th April 2008 onwards.

Individual circumstances vary so it's also always vital to get professional advice before you do anything that may have tax consequences.

After reading this guide, however, we are confident that you will have a firm grasp of how capital gains tax is calculated and what you can do to pay less of it when you sell your properties.

As for jargon, there isn't very much of it you'll be pleased to hear.

We sometimes refer to capital gains tax as just CGT. You may also see us talk about the 'taxman' when referring to HM Revenue & Customs, also known as HMRC.

Tax is all about tax years and some of the examples have dates in them. The UK is one of the few remaining countries that insists on having a tax year which doesn't run from January to December. Our tax year runs from 6th April in one year to 5th April the next year.

Chapter 2

Just How Bad is Capital Gains Tax?

Capital gains tax can be a serious burden but this can be mitigated through the many exemptions and reliefs which are available.

For starters the first £9,600 of your annual capital gains are completely tax free. Couples enjoy one capital gains tax exemption each so they can enjoy £19,200 tax free every year.

Whatever's left over will be taxed at just 18%.

Example

So let's say you and your spouse or partner sell a property and make a £20,000 profit. The first £19,200 will be covered by your two annual exemptions and the remaining £800 will be taxed at 18%, producing a tax bill of just £144. What this means is that your actual tax rate is just 1%:

Profit	Tax	Tax Rate
£20,000	£144	1%

Clearly, earning £20,000 of capital gains is a lot better than earning an extra £20,000 of income, especially if you're paying 40% income tax. Income tax on £20,000 could be as much as £8,000.

Here are some more examples of effective capital gains tax rates for married couples and others who own property with a partner. They're calculated by deducting two annual exemptions and taxing the remaining profits at 18%:

Profit	Tax	Tax Rate
£50,000	£5,544	11%
£100,000	£14,544	15%
£250,000	£41,544	17%

Clearly, paying tax at a rate of 11%, 15% or 17% is quite attractive compared with the tax you would have to pay on other income and investments.

However, £14,000 or £41,000 is still a lot of tax, but the good news is there are lots of things you can do to reduce your capital gains tax bill... as we'll see shortly.

Chapter 3

How Capital Gains Tax is Calculated

Before we look at strategies you can follow to reduce your capital gains tax bill it's important to explain exactly how the tax is calculated.

CGT can be extremely complex... but it can also be extremely simple.

To show you how it's calculated, we're going to look at a property investor called Kate who sells a buy-to-let flat. We'll keep tax terminology and jargon to the bare minimum for now because it gets in the way of understanding how capital gains tax is calculated.

Now let's say Kate bought the flat two years ago for £200,000 and sells it for £250,000. So she has made a profit of £50,000.

However she probably doesn't have to pay tax on the whole £50,000 because this is not her true net profit.

She will probably have racked up some costs when she sold the property, such as solicitor's fees, estate agent fees and advertising.

She will also have paid some costs when she originally bought the property, for example survey fees, stamp duty and more solicitors fees.

These direct costs of buying and selling the property can be deducted when calculating her capital gains tax. Let's say her total selling costs are £3,000 and her buying costs were also £3,000. Her net gain is now calculated as follows:

	£
Sales proceeds	250,000
Less: Purchase price	200,000
Less: Selling costs	3,000
Less: Purchase costs	3,000
Net Gain	**44,000**

We're almost finished. To calculate her CGT bill all we have to do is deduct her annual capital gains tax exemption which is currently £9,600. So Kate's final taxable profit (also known as her 'chargeable gain') is £34,400:

Chargeable gain = £44,000 - £9,600 = £34,400

and her final capital gains tax bill will be £6,192:

£34,400 x 18% = £6,192

In summary, Kate made a £50,000 'profit' selling her flat and after deducting her buying and selling costs and annual CGT exemption is left with a tax bill of around £6,000.

You may be interested to know that under the old capital gains tax rules Kate's tax bill could have been almost £14,000 – over twice as much!

Keeping Good Documentation

Before we move on I'd like to make one small point about documentation.

When you come to sell your property it's important to have evidence of all your purchase costs, proving how much you spent on legal fees, stamp duty and so on. If you bought the property many years ago this is often easier said than done.

That's why it's imperative, whenever you buy a property, to keep hold of all the documentation showing your various purchase costs.

One easy solution is to always keep a separate ring file which contains all the important documentation for every property you own. File your purchase receipts in there and you should be able to dig them out 10 or even 20 years later!

Improvements

Apart from her buying and selling costs Kate can also claim a tax deduction for any improvements she made to the property. Why? Because if your property goes up in value by £5,000 after you spend £5,000 improving it, you haven't really made a profit and therefore shouldn't be taxed.

So for every £1 you spend on improvements you can reduce your chargeable gain by £1.

Let's say Kate spent £5,000 on some improvements to the property, such as installing an en-suite bathroom in one of the bedrooms. Kate's calculation now looks like this:

	£
Sales proceeds	250,000
Less: Purchase price	200,000
Less: Selling costs	3,000
Less: Purchase costs	3,000
Less: Improvements	5,000
Less: CGT exemption	9,600
Chargeable gain	29,400
Tax @ 18%	5,292

So by remembering to claim her improvement costs Kate has cut her tax bill by £900.

So what exactly are improvements? They're often confused with repairs which are treated completely differently. We'll return to this issue later.

Summary

That believe it or not is as complicated as many property capital gains tax calculations get.

You simply take your basic profit which is found by subtracting the purchase price from the selling price.

You then deduct all your:

- Buying costs
- Selling costs
- Improvements
- Annual capital gains tax exemption

Finally, whatever's left is your taxable profit. Multiply by 18% and you have your tax bill.

Some Extra Buying and Selling Costs

We mentioned that some of the costs you can deduct include:

- Solicitors fees – buying and selling
- Estate agent fees
- Stamp duty
- Survey fees
- Advertising
- Improvements

Another cost you can deduct for capital gains tax is any money you spent defending your property from legal attack. A good example would be legal fees as a result of a boundary dispute.

Apart from your actual improvements you can also deduct any professional fees you incur to obtain planning permission for them.

A Quick Point about Mortgages

A lot of property investors make the mistake of thinking their outstanding mortgage can be deducted when calculating capital gains tax. Mortgages have absolutely nothing to do with capital gains tax and shouldn't feature anywhere in your calculation.

Of course mortgage interest for buy-to-let properties can be claimed as an income tax deduction when you do your annual income tax return. But that's entirely separate from capital gains tax.

Proceeds and Base Cost

To keep things simple in Kate's case, we simply subtracted all of her buying and selling costs and improvements.

The formal tax calculation that you see in textbooks and manuals is a bit different. The taxman does the calculation by separating your expenses into two different groups.

Your selling costs are subtracted from the sale price of the property. This gives us your 'proceeds'.

The buying costs and improvement costs are added to the original purchase price of the property. This gives us your 'base cost'.

Your gain is then calculated by subtracting your base cost from your proceeds:

Gain = Proceeds – Base cost

As before, you then subtract your annual CGT exemption and whatever's left is taxed at 18%.

The result is exactly the same as before but you may need to know what your proceeds and base cost are when completing your tax return or when reading literature from the Revenue and Customs website or when communicating with your accountant.

Chapter 4

Paying Capital Gains Tax &
Completing Your Return

Paying Your Tax

We now know how much capital gains tax Kate has to pay – the question is, when does she have to pay it?

Let's say she sold the property on June 1st 2008.

That means the sale falls into the tax year which ends on 5th April 2009.

Kate then has to pay her tax by 31st January 2010, the deadline for submitting electronic tax returns for that year.

Unlike income tax you don't have to pay instalments of capital gains tax throughout the year.

What You Have to Report to the Taxman

In the vast majority of cases you will have to tell the taxman about any property you sell when you fill in your tax return.

However, there are a couple of exceptions. For example, you don't have to report the sale on your tax return:

- If there's no tax to pay and your proceeds are less than four times the annual CGT exemption:

  4 x £9,600 = £38,400

  So if you sell a property for less than £38,400 and your profit is tax free because it's covered by the annual exemption, you don't have to report it on your tax return.

Of course there aren't many properties that sell for as little as £38,400 these days. It's mainly share investors who can take advantage of this concession.

However, if you're part of a group or syndicate of investors who own a property, then you could find yourself in this favourable position.

• You also don't have to report sales of property that are fully covered by your principal private residence exemption. In other words, most times when you sell your home you don't have to tell the taxman about it.

Having said all that, the vast majority of property investors have to report their sales on their tax returns. You do this by completing what's known as the *Capital Gains Summary*. This form can usually be downloaded by typing "sa108.pdf" into Google or from this web address:

http://www.hmrc.gov.uk/forms/sa108.pdf

However, be careful to make sure that the form you download is in fact the correct one for the tax year in question. Alternatively, you can get the form by calling the HMRC helpline: 0845 9000 404.

How to Complete Your Tax Return

Completing the capital gains tax pages isn't difficult once you've done the number crunching.

There are currently just two pages and not all of the boxes have to be filled in. However, you do have to send in your computations, along with the form.

To show you how to report a property sale on your tax return we've uploaded a sample completed capital gains tax form. It's based on Kate's sale and you'll find it at this web address.

www.taxcafe.co.uk/katecgt

We're confident that when you go through it you will agree with those awful TV adverts that tax doesn't have to be taxing!

Please note, however, that we've used the **current** capital gains tax form for the 2007/8 tax year in this example.

The new one for sales taking place after April 6th 2008 has not been published yet and won't be until 2009.

Nevertheless this sample form will give you a good grasp of how to report property sales on your tax return.

Chapter 5

Capital Gains Tax - The Big 7

The example with Kate is about as simple as it gets. We'll take a look at some of the complexities that arise shortly.

First of all I'd like to spend a couple of minutes going through what I call the Big Seven.

These are seven basic but very important facts about capital gains tax which every property investor should know.

Rule #1
Only UK Residents Pay Capital Gains Tax

Most people living in the UK fall into the capital gains tax net. However, you do not have to pay capital gains tax if you are non resident.

So if you want to escape capital gains tax altogether all you have to do is emigrate. We'll take a look at the emigration rules later on.

Companies also don't pay capital gains tax – instead they pay corporation tax when they sell properties.

So the information contained here is aimed mainly at people, not companies, who are UK resident.

Rule #2
How You Use the Property is What Matters

A property can be used in lots of different ways. How you use it determines how it is taxed when you sell.

For example, you may buy the property to:

• Keep as your main residence	No capital gains tax
• Use as a 2nd home	Capital gains tax
• Use in your business	Capital gains tax
• Rent out ('buy to let')	Capital gains tax
• Develop for profit	Income tax
• Sell on for a profit	Income tax

Generally speaking, the only time you can escape tax altogether is when the property is your main residence. If you own property for any other purpose your profits will be taxed.

The question then is, do I have to pay income tax or capital gains tax? There's a massive difference between the two taxes. Income tax could be as high as 40%, compared with 18% for capital gains tax. The other advantage of paying CGT is the annual exemption which shelters the first £9,600 of your profits from the taxman.

As a general rule if you buy a property with the intention of renovating or developing it and selling it for a profit you are a trader and your profits are subject to income tax.

The same applies if you're a speculator, for example if you buy a property at a good price and your dominant reason for buying it was to sell at a profit.

However, if you buy a property to rent out or as a second home you will be subject to capital gains tax.

There are plenty of grey areas and in practice you may have more than one objective when you buy a property. Properties can also be used for more than one purpose.

Let's look at an example.

Example

Let's say Anne bought an old farmhouse. She lived in the property for three months and then moved out while substantial renovation work took place. After the work was completed, she let it out for six months.

Halfway through the period of the lease she put the property on the market and sold it.

This is what one would call 'borderline'. Anne has had some personal use out of the property and has let it out, but she has also developed it and sold it after only a short period of ownership.

This case would warrant a much closer look at all of the circumstances. It should be decided on the basis of Anne's intentions but who, apart from Anne herself, would ever know what these truly were?

Such a case could go either way. The more Anne can do to demonstrate that her intention had been to hold the property as a long-term investment, the better her chances of claiming capital gains tax treatment.

Her personal and financial circumstances will be crucial. For example, if she had got married around the time of the sale, or had got into unexpected financial difficulties, which had forced her to make the sale, then she might successfully argue for capital gains tax treatment.

Rule #3
It Doesn't Matter <u>How Long</u> You Own the Property

Before taper relief was abolished it did matter how long you owned the property. The longer you owned it, the less tax you paid.

Not any more. As long as the property is initially bought as a long-term investment, then whether you own it for one year or 30 years you pay tax at the same rate – 18%.

Most buy-to-let landlords are long-term investors. However, the new capital gains tax rules are great news for the slightly more aggressive investor who tends to sell properties regularly.

For example, you may wish to sell a buy-to-let property in one location and invest in another more profitable area. In the past you would have had to pay as much as 40% in capital gains tax. Now you only pay 18%.

Rule #4
It Doesn't Matter **<u>What Type</u>** of Property You Own

Until recently different types of property had different capital gains tax rates. In particular, many commercial properties qualified for business asset taper relief. This entitled them to a 10% tax rate.

That's all history. From now on it doesn't matter what type of property you own – the capital gains tax rate is 18% for all property including:

- Buy-to-let flats and houses
- Holiday homes
- Commercial shops, offices, and warehouses

There are only two exceptions to this rule. Furnished holiday lets in the UK qualify for the new Entrepreneurs Relief which allows gains of up to £1 million to be taxed at just 10%. Business owners who sell their trading premises when they sell their business can also qualify for this relief. More about this later.

Rule #5
You Generally Cannot Avoid Tax by Reinvesting

A common question we at Taxcafe get asked is whether you can avoid capital gains tax by buying another property.

For the vast majority of property investors the answer is No.

There are however a couple of types of property that do qualify for this concession. These are:

- Property used as your business trading premises
- Furnished holiday lets in the UK

This concession is called rollover relief and we'll talk about it a bit more later on.

All other types of property, be it residential or commercial, are taxed when you sell them.

Rule #6
It Doesn't Matter <u>Where</u> You Invest

This has always been the rule but it's worth emphasising now that overseas property investment is so incredibly popular.

UK capital gains tax applies to all your properties, whether they're in the UK or abroad.

Some overseas countries have their own capital gains tax, others do not – it doesn't really matter as far as the UK taxman is concerned. You still fall into the UK capital gains tax net.

We see a lot of brochures advertising overseas property investments. Sometimes they say things like "No Capital Gains Tax". Remember that's overseas capital gains tax they're talking about. There may not be any capital gains tax in the country where the property is located but you still have to pay UK capital gains tax when you sell.

However, you don't have to worry about paying tax twice. The general rule is that any tax you pay overseas is allowed as a credit against your UK capital gains tax bill.

Rule #7
It Doesn't Matter How Much Income You Earn

This is something new. In the past your capital gains tax depended on how much other income you earned. As a result you could have ended up paying tax at just 20% or even 10%. Only higher-rate tax payers paid 40% on everything.

The new 18% tax rate applies to everyone – which is very good news for higher-rate taxpayers but not such good news for many basic-rate tax payers.

Summary – The Big 7

Let's just summarize those rules again because they're very important:

- If you're UK resident or ordinarily resident you fall into the capital gains tax net. If you emigrate you can avoid CGT altogether.

- All property profits are taxed in some way, unless the property is your main residence.

- You'll pay income tax if you're actively developing or trading any type of property.

- Most other properties are subject to capital gains tax, including buy to lets, holiday homes, shops, and offices.

- Capital gains tax is the same for all these properties although tax can be postponed on UK furnished holiday lets and property used in your business.

- Furnished holiday lets and trading premises may also be taxed at a lower rate thanks to the new Entrepreneurs Relief.

- It doesn't matter how long you hold onto a property from now on – the tax rate will be the same whether it's one year or one decade.

- Overseas properties are no exception – they still fall into the UK tax net.

- It doesn't matter whether you're a pauper or a billionaire – all property investors pay capital gains tax at the same flat rate of 18%.

Chapter 6

More Complex Issues and Jargon

Not all capital gains tax calculations are as simple as Kate's buy-to-let flat. In this section we're going to look at some of the nitty-gritty rules you may also have to be aware of.

They don't apply to all property sales but where they do apply they're important.

The Date of the Sale

Let's kick off with dates. Establishing the exact date of a property sale can be important. For example, you may have to work out whether a sale falls into the current tax year or a later year.

For capital gains tax purposes the sale is treated as taking place as soon as there is an **unconditional contract**. It's important to note that this may be earlier than the completion date of the sale.

For example, let's say James completes the sale of an investment property on 8th April 2009. James thinks he only has to pay capital gains tax by 31st January 2011.

However, let's say the unconditional sale contract was signed on 1st April 2009 – in other words, just before the end of the previous tax year. The capital gains tax due will be payable by 31st January 2010 – 12 months earlier than he originally hoped.

So as you can see, establishing the exact date of sale can be important for tax purposes.

Sales to Friends and Family

You should also be aware that sometimes the actual selling price of the property is not used to calculate your capital gains tax.

Why? Because people sometimes try to give property for nothing to close family and friends to escape capital gains tax ... or sell it for much less than it's worth.

If a property is sold for much less than it's worth, there will be little or no profit and therefore no capital gains tax to pay. That's the theory anyway. Unfortunately the taxman doesn't always see it that way.

The legal term for transactions between close family and associates is:

'Not at arm's length'

There are two types of property sales of this nature which the taxman is on the look out for:

Type 1 – Connected Persons

The first is sales or gifts to 'connected persons'. Connected persons include most of your close family:

- Husbands, wives and civil partners
- Mothers, fathers
- Grandparents, great grandparents etc
- Sons, daughters, grandchildren, great grandchildren and so on
- Brothers or sisters
- In-laws
- Business partners
- Any company you or any of the above people control
- A trust where any of the above are beneficiaries

Sales or gifts between 'connected' persons are treated as taking place at the **full open market value of the property**.

So even if you sell a £1 million property to your brother for just £1 you'll still have to pay capital gains tax as if you had sold it for £1 million.

You have to be very careful when you give away properties which are sitting on big profits. You'll still have to pay capital gains tax but, because there are no sales proceeds, you may not have any cash to pay the tax bill.

In fact cash is often the best asset to give away because this never results in a CGT bill (except foreign currency sometimes). Failing that you should try to give away assets that haven't appreciated in value much.

Type 2 – Other Sales Not at Arm's Length

Apart from sales to close family there are other sales that are also not at arm's length. The result is the same as before – open market value is used instead of the actual sales price. Examples include:

- Transfers between unmarried partners
- Sales of properties to your employees
- A sale which is just part of a larger transaction or a series of transactions

Point 3 may look a little confusing but what the taxman is trying to prevent is people selling assets for less than they're worth and getting some other type of indirect kickback or payment.

Burden of Proof

There's an important difference between these sales and sales between connected family members.

Where sales take place between connected family members it is **automatically assumed** that the transaction is not at arm's length and market value is substituted for the actual sales price.

Where the transaction isn't between connected persons, it's up to Revenue and Customs to prove that the sale is not at arm's length – there is no automatic assumption that this is the case.

In reality, of course, it can be difficult for the taxman to prove whether properties are sold for less than they're worth. If you give your house to your common law partner for nothing, it's clear this is a transaction not at arm's length. But if you sell the property for only slightly less than it would have fetched on the open market it would be more difficult for the taxman to prove anything.

The only way to truly establish what a property's worth is to sell it on the open market. Failing that you have to get it valued and valuations can easily differ by 10% or even 20%.

Sales Not for Cash

Sometimes people sell property and instead of getting cash they may get paid with other assets. In these cases to calculate your CGT you take the market value of the assets you've been given.

Example

Let's take an extremely simple example. Let's say you sell your holiday home in exchange for stock market shares worth £150,000.

When you come to do your capital gains tax calculation for disposing of your house, your proceeds will be the market value of the quoted shares you've been given, namely £150,000.

The Cost of Your Property

Usually the cost figure used in your capital gains tax calculation is the amount you paid for the property. However, there are a couple of special situations where the cost is determined using something else.

Inherited Properties

For example, if you inherit a property and later sell it, the cost used in the CGT calculation is the market value at the date of the previous owner's death:

Capital gain = Sales price − Market value at death

For example, let's say a father died and left his son a property that was valued at £150,000 for probate purposes. The son sells the property for £200,000 in August 2008.

The capital gain is calculated as follows:

Capital gain = £200,000 - £150,000 = £50,000

The son only pays tax on the profit made since he owned it.

Properties Acquired From Spouses

If a husband gives his wife a property there's no capital gains tax. However, when the wife eventually sells the property she has to use her husband's base cost.

For example, let's say Fiona gives her husband Alan a property worth £200,000 which she bought for £100,000.

Because they're married there's no capital gains tax payable. Alan later sells it for £300,000. His capital gain is the price he sold it for minus what Fiona originally paid for it:

Capital gain = £300,000 - £100,000 = £200,000

Properties Bought Before 31 March 1982

Another example where you don't use the actual cost of the property in the CGT calculation concerns properties you acquired before the end of March 1982. So this one's for those of you out there who've been in the property game for a long time!

For these properties you have to use the market value on March 31st 1982. Many surveyors are well accustomed to providing 'March 1982' valuations but this is becoming more of a hypothetical exercise as time goes by.

Summary

Well that's the end of the section which explains some of the special cases you have to watch out for when calculating capital gains tax.

In summary:

- Your sale takes place as soon as there is a binding contract. This is the date used in your CGT calculation. It's not necessarily the completion date of the sale.

- If you sell or give a property to a connected person (usually close family) you have to pay tax on the full open market value.

- There are other sales not at arm's length you should watch out for.

- If someone pays you in kind instead of in cash, to calculate your CGT you use the market value of the assets you've been given.

- If you sell a property you inherited, use the probate value of the property as your cost.

- If your spouse gives you a property there is no CGT payable. However, when you eventually sell the property, use your spouse's original cost when calculating your CGT.

Next we're going to discuss the main residence exemption which protects you from the taxman when you sell your home.

Chapter 7

The Principal Private Residence Exemption

When you sell your home the profit is tax free – most of us know that.

Not many people realise just how far this tax loophole can be pushed. For example, it can be used, not just by homeowners, but by property investors as well.

The formal name for this tax relief is the Principal Private Residence exemption, also known as PPR.

Climbing the Property Ladder

Because profits on your home are completely tax free, it usually makes sense to keep climbing the property ladder during your working life, buying bigger and better homes to live in.

One day you can sell up and downsize. Alternatively, you may wish to retire to a cheaper part of the country. By replacing your expensive home with a cheaper one you can get your hands on a cash lump sum which is completely tax free.

Many people do this to boost their pension savings.

Some DIY enthusiasts use the main residence tax shelter much more aggressively than this. What they do is buy a property in need of repair and live in it for a couple of years while they do it up. They then sell up and move on to the next project. The profit they make from doing up the property will usually be completely tax free.

Some would argue that doing up a house and selling it for a healthy profit is a lot more lucrative than, say, taking a part time job.

Renting Out Your Old Home

The principal private residence exemption can also be used by buy-to-let investors to earn tax-free profits.

This is because there's a special PPR rule which applies to all properties that have been your main residence at some time in the past.

What this rule says is that the last 3 years you own the property are always tax free. And it doesn't matter how you use the property during those last 3 years.

In other words, you can move out of your home, rent it out for three years, and still not pay a penny in capital gains tax.

As long as you've lived in the property as your main residence at some point in the past you qualify for this tax break.

Example

Naz buys a flat in Docklands and makes it his home. He then buys a new home in Mayfair and decides to rent out the Docklands flat. Three years later he sells the Docklands flat for a £200,000 profit.

In this example, the profit is completely tax free – the property qualifies for the principal private residence exemption because it used to be his home and he sold it within 3 years of moving out.

Here's another example how this rule can be put to good use.

Example

Neil lives in a block of flats. He buys a second flat in the block as an investment. Now he has two choices. He can either rent out the new flat or move into it and rent out the old flat.

Let's say he decides to stay where he is and rent out the new property. Three years later he sells it and makes a £100,000 profit.

His capital gains tax bill could be as much as £18,000:

$$£100,000 \times 18\% = £18,000$$

Let's say he decides instead to move into the new property and rent out his old flat. What will the capital gains tax bill be when he sells the old flat in 3 years time?

Because this property used to be his main residence, the last three years of ownership are completely tax free so Neil's capital gains tax bill is zero!

What this proves is that old homes are much better tax shelters than ordinary buy-to-let properties. It's a mouth-watering tax break and one that should be made use of whenever the opportunity arises.

Calculating Your PPR

So how do you calculate your principal private residence exemption when you do your tax return? It's quite simple and best illustrated with an example.

Let's say Dave has a net gain on a buy to let property of £100,000.

He has owned the property for 10 years. He lived in it for one year and rented it out for the rest.

How much is tax free?

Thanks to the final three years rule he gets 4 years of PPR – the 1 year he lived in it plus the 3 bonus years. This means that 4 out of 10 years are tax free. In other words 40% of his profits are tax free.

His PPR exemption is:

$$£100,000 \times 40\% = £40,000$$

On a technical note it's worth pointing out that the £100,000 profit is his net profit after deducting all of his buying and selling costs and improvements.

In practice, all capital gains tax calculations must be carried out more accurately, in days rather than years, but the results are much the same.

Private Letting Relief

Let's say you decide to hold onto your old home for more than three years. The final three years will still be tax free but the additional years may be taxable.

However, there's another capital gains tax relief which comes to the rescue in these situations called Private Letting Relief.

To get private letting relief there are two conditions. The property must have been:

- Your main residence at some time, and
- Rented out as private residential accommodation at some time.

It's essential that you rented out the property. A property that has simply been left vacant won't qualify.

So How Much is Private Letting Relief Worth?

The absolute maximum you can get is a tax deduction of £40,000. In other words £40,000 of your profits will escape capital gains tax.

However, if you sell more than one property in the same tax year you're allowed £40,000 for each and every property.

As long as the property is a former main residence which you rented out it qualifies for this tax relief.

It gets even better than this. Each owner of the property qualifies for this relief. So a couple may be able to shelter up to £80,000 of their profits per property from the taxman.

Calculating Your Private Letting Relief

The exact amount of private letting relief you get is calculated by looking at three numbers:

1. Your PPR exemption for the property
2. The capital gain made while the property was let out
3. £40,000

Your deduction is the **smallest** of these three numbers.

Point 1 is simple to understand – we've just showed you how to calculate your PPR exemption. Point 3 is also simple to understand – it's just a number!

Point 2 is essentially the net profit while you were renting out the property. For example, if you own a property for 10 years and rent it out for the first five, then this number will be half your gain from the property.

The only quirk which you have to watch is that this number cannot include the last three years. Why – because those last three years are covered by your PPR exemption anyway.

It's important to remember that we use the smallest of the three numbers when calculating your private letting relief.

Detailed Example

Let's briefly run through an example which shows how easy capital gains tax calculations are even if you introduce extra reliefs like the principal private residence exemption (PPR) and private letting relief and also to show you how powerful these reliefs can be in helping you pay less capital gains tax.

Let's say Amanda bought a nice little flat in London for £200,000. She spent £19,000 improving it and lived in it for just one year. Her employer then transferred her to the firm's Edinburgh office and she decided to keep the flat and rent it out. Six years later Amanda sells it for £400,000.

So how much tax does she pay? She has doubled her money but is worried there will be a big capital gains tax bill because she only lived in the property for 1 out of the 7 years she owned it.

Assuming her buying and selling costs were £3,000 each, her capital gains tax calculation goes like this:

	£
Sales proceeds	400,000
Less: Purchase price	200,000
Less: Selling costs	3,000
Less: Purchase costs	3,000
Less: Improvements	19,000
Net gain	**175,000**

The next step is calculating the various reliefs Amanda is entitled to. She lived in the property as her main residence so she qualifies for the PPR exemption. She lived there for just one year but remember she also gets the last 3 years. So in total 4 out of the 7 years are tax free.

To calculate her PPR we simply multiply her net gain by 4/7

$$4/7 \times £175,000 = £100,000$$

This figure is her PPR exemption which she can deduct from her net gain.

Next we calculate her private letting relief. We know she has lived in the property *and* rented it out so she does qualify for this relief. It's the smallest of these three numbers:

- Her PPR exemption which we know is £100,000
- Her gain during the letting period
- £40,000

How do we calculate her gain during the letting period? Well we know her total gain is £175,000 and we know the property was rented out for 6 out of the 7 years she owned it.

However, we don't count the last 3 years because that overlaps with her PPR exemption. So in this case the gain during the letting period is calculated as follows:

$$£175,000 \times 3/7 = £75,000$$

It's the smallest number that we use, so Amanda can claim £40,000 in private letting relief.

Finally, she can deduct her annual capital gains tax exemption and whatever's left over is taxed at 18%

In summary, Amanda's capital gains tax calculation looks like this:

	£
Sales proceeds	400,000
Less:	
Purchase price	200,000
Selling costs	3,000
Purchase costs	3,000
Improvements	19,000
Net gain	**175,000**
Less:	
PPR 4/7 x £175,000	100,000
Private letting relief	40,000
Annual CGT exemption	9,600
Chargeable gain	25,400
Tax @18%	**4,572**

Just over £4,500 in tax is not a bad result when you consider that she made a profit of £175,000 on the property. Her effective tax rate is just 2.6%!

Remember the PPR exemption and private letting relief can only be claimed when a property has been your main residence at some time in the past.

Before we move on it's important to answer some of the most frequently asked questions about main residences and tax.

What is Your Main Residence?

This is an important issue especially if you have more than one home. Your main residence is tax free but what exactly is your main residence?

- For starters, only one property can be your main residence at any point in time.

- That property can be located anywhere in the world – it doesn't necessarily have to be in the UK.

- To qualify for the PPR exemption the property must usually have been physically occupied as your home. In other words, if you never live in the property it generally can't be your main residence, even if it's the only property you own.

- You don't have to live there permanently, however. Your occupation can be occasional and short which is why a holiday house can qualify as your main residence'

- Of course you can only have one main residence at a time so if you decide it's to be your holiday house in, say, Spain then your house in the UK will no longer qualify and will no longer be completely tax free.

- You can rent out a holiday house some of the time and still claim it as your primary residence... there will, however, be a reduction in the amount of PPR relief available.

- If you have more than one home you can choose which one is your main residence but you must follow a special procedure to do this. More on that later.

- Finally, a property doesn't have to be conventional bricks and mortar – caravans, houseboats etc may all qualify for the PPR exemption.

What about Couples?

Each unmarried individual can have one main residence.

This means an unmarried couple can have two tax-free main residences – one each.

Of course the other requirements still stand – meaning each property must be lived in by the owner.

Married couples, however, can only have one main residence covered by the principal private residence exemption. The same goes for civil partnerships.

If a married couple own two private residences they then have to decide which one is the main residence.

How Long Do You Have to Live in the Property?

This is a question we get asked all the time at Taxcafe.

How long do you have to live in a property so that is qualifies for the principal private residence exemption?

There is no 'hard and fast' rule. What we usually say is that it's the **quality** of occupation that counts, not the length. It's recommended that you:

- Move into the property for a substantial period.

- Ensure that all relevant institutions (banks, utilities, Revenue & Customs, etc) are notified.

- Inform your family and friends.

- Furnish the property for permanent occupation.

- Register on the electoral roll at that address.

- Do not advertise the property for sale or rent until after the expiry of a substantial period.

It's not possible to provide a definitive view of what would be a 'substantial period'. What matters is that the property genuinely becomes your 'permanent home' for a period.

As a rough guide only, you should plan your affairs on the basis that you will be residing in the property for at least a year. Where you are looking to use the principal private residence exemption you must occupy that property completely wholeheartedly – a mere 'sham' occupation will not suffice.

What if I'm Away from Home Temporarily?

Your PPR exemption remains intact during certain periods of absence from the property. These include:

- Up to 3 years – regardless of the reason
- Up to 4 years – if you're working elsewhere in the UK
- No limit – if you're working abroad.

As regards point 1, the three year period can be made up of either one period or lots of short periods.

As regards, the second two points, it doesn't matter whether it's you or your spouse who has to work away from home. However, to protect your PPR exemption you have to make sure you:

- Occupy the property as your main residence both before and after you are absent from the property, and

- Do not own any other property which could be treated as your main residence.

What if a Relative Lives in the Property?

A common question is whether you can claim the PPR exemption for a dependent relative who lives in a property you own. Only in limited circumstances is this possible – most notably the property must have been occupied by your relative before 6th April 1988.

In a nutshell, most people cannot claim this exemption.

What Happens if I Rent Out Part of My Home?

If you take on one lodger it is generally accepted that this will not harm your PPR exemption. A lodger is someone who has their own room but otherwise shares the house.

If you rent out part of your house under other circumstances it's likely to harm your PPR exemption. However, as long as there are no permanent alterations to the structure of the property, you will probably still get quite a lot of relief.

Example

For example, let's say you divide your two storey house into two flats – you live in the lower half and rent out the upper half. Before you sell it you convert it back into one house which you occupy.

Let's say after owning the property for 10 years you sell it and your gain is £200,000.

The gain of £100,000 for the lower half that you lived in is fully covered by your PPR exemption and tax free.

But what about the £100,000 gain on the upper half that was rented out?

Let's say you lived in the whole house for 2 years before converting it into flats. The gain of £100,000 on the upper half is fully covered for the first 2 years when you lived in it AND, thanks to that special rule, the last 3 years – a total of 5 of the 10 years.

So half of the £100,000 gain on the upper half is tax free – leaving £50,000 taxable.

That's not all, however. You also qualify for private letting relief. We won't go through the calculation in this example but the amount you can claim is £40,000, which leaves you with a taxable gain of only £10,000.

You can then deduct your annual CGT exemption (currently £9,600) leaving just £400 taxed at 18%.

All in all, you'll end up paying just £72 tax on your £100,000 gain!

What if I Use Part of My Home for Business?

This is a common scenario. Many taxpayers use a room in their house to run a business – including their property letting business.

If you do this you can claim lots of income tax deductions each year including a proportion of your council tax, mortgage interest, utilities and so on.

However, you have to be cautious if you do this because if that room is used **exclusively** for business purposes then the PPR exemption is not available for that part of your home.

The way to get around this is to ensure that the room is not used exclusively for business purposes. You should restrict your income tax claim to say 99% of the office's running costs. For example you could ensure that the office also doubles up as:

- A guest bedroom
- Storage for personal belongings
- A library

Doing this could save you a lot in future capital gains tax but won't have much effect on your income tax claim.

Second Homes

Lots of people have second homes, either in the UK or overseas. But in most cases only one of your homes is covered by your PPR exemption. The other home falls into the capital gains tax net.

Most people keep the status quo and the house they live in most of the time is also their main residence for tax purposes.

This is not necessarily a good idea, however. Sometimes it pays to have your second home treated as your main residence in order to save capital gains tax.

The good news is you can pick and choose which of your homes is to be treated as your tax-free main residence. How do you do that? Within two years of acquiring a second property you can **elect** to make it your main residence.

Furthermore, this election will apply from the date your second property first became available to you as a private residence – usually from the day you bought it.

Example

Let's say Mark lives in a flat in London which he bought a year ago. He then buys a second home in Wales where he spends many long weekends and holidays.

Just under two years later, he realises that his Welsh house has gone up in value a lot more than his London flat. He therefore elects his Welsh house as his main residence. This election automatically applies from the day that Mark first had two residences so, in effect, the Welsh property is tax free since the day he bought it.

Now let's move forward in time. Three years after making the main residence election Mark sells the Welsh house at a substantial gain. This gain is totally tax free because he has elected that property as his principal private residence.

What about Mark's London flat? This has not been his main residence since the day he purchased the Welsh property, five years ago. Remember, the main residence election applies to the Welsh property from day one.

Although the London flat hasn't been his main residence for the last five years, it was his main residence for one year before that. So if he sells it now his final three years of ownership will also be tax free thanks to the special three-year rule.

Let's look at the overall tax position on the two properties:

- Starting with the Welsh house, this is totally tax free because the PPR election covered it from day one.

- And what about the London flat? Mark has owned this property for 6 years. It was his main residence for the first year and so tax free during that time. After that the Welsh house became Mark's main residence for the remaining five years. However, the last three of those are also tax free. So 4 out of 6 years, or two thirds, of Mark's gain on his London flat is tax free.

But Mark could have done better than this.

Once you have a main residence election in place (within the critical two year time limit) you can change your election at any time. Furthermore, the new election can be back-dated by up to two years. Let's return to our example to see how this helps.

Example Revisited

As soon as Mark decided that he was going to sell his Welsh house, he made a new main residence election in favour of his London flat and back-dated it by two years.

Let's say it then took six months before the sale of the Welsh house was completed.

This means that the Welsh house ceased to be Mark's main residence 2½ years before he sold it.

However, we know that any former main residence is also exempt for the last 3 years, so the Welsh house is still totally tax-free!

How has this helped?

The London flat now gains an extra 2½ years as Mark's main residence.

Let's say Mark then sells the London flat 3 years later, after he has owned it for a total of 9 years. The flat then qualifies as his main residence for 6½ years out of 9 (the first year and the last 5½).

If Mark had not bothered to change his main residence election and had left things as they stood, his London flat would only have qualified for exemption for 4 out of the 9 years.

The rule is this: if you have two or more residences and expect to sell your main residence within a year, you should make a back-dated election in favour of one of your other residences.

But remember, you can only do this if you made your original main residence election within that critical two year period.

So Which Property Should You Elect as Your Main Residence?

The important point to remember is that it's not necessarily your most valuable property that should be your main residence for tax purposes – it's the property that is rising in value the fastest.

For example, let's say you have two properties:

- A house in the city worth £400,000, rising in value by £15,000 per year.

- A cottage in the country worth £150,000 but rising in value by £30,000 per year.

Clearly you should elect to treat the cottage as your main residence even though it's not your most valuable property. Why? Because it's generating more profit than the city house and those profits will be taxed unless you make the election.

The great thing about this election is you don't have to gamble – you can wait almost two years to see which property has risen in value the most and choose that property as your main residence.

It's also important to remember that once you make a main residence election you're not stuck with it – it can be changed at any time and you can backdate those changes by up to two years.

In fact you can apply this strategy to as many properties as you like. For example, if you're lucky enough to have five holiday homes, you can elect to make any one of them your main residence at any time.

And remember all of these properties will then be tax free for the last three years you own them.

Why You Should Always Make an Election

Many people with a second home find that their main home is in fact the most valuable **and** is also increasing in value the fastest. At first glance, it seems obvious that the main home should then remain your main residence for capital gains tax purposes.

However, there are two very important reasons why you should still make a main residence election when you acquire a second home:

- Firstly, making an election within two years of buying your second home preserves your right to change the election later on. So if it ever begins to look like you would prefer your second home to be your main residence, you will still have that option.

- Secondly, a main residence election in favour of your second home can be quickly changed to your main home. Revenue and Customs' own manuals say you can make this change just one week later.

So, if you do this you sacrifice just one week of exemption on your main home but your second home gains three things:

- Main residence status for one week

- More importantly, main residence exemption for the last three years of your ownership

- Finally, you will also get private letting relief if you ever subsequently rent it out. Remember this relief is only available if the property has been your main residence.

So that's three years of exemption and possibly up to another £40,000 of relief in exchange for losing just one week of exemption on your main home.

The rule is: always, **always, <u>always</u>** make a main residence election when you buy a second home.

How Do You Make a Main Residence Election?

Making a main residence election is simple. The election must be made in writing, addressed to 'Her Majesty's Inspector of Taxes' and sent to your tax office. An unmarried individual must sign the election personally in order for it to be effective. A married couple or civil partnership must both sign the election.

There is no particular prescribed form for the election, although the following example wording would be suitable for inclusion:

"In accordance with section 222(5) Taxation of Chargeable Gains Act 1992, [I/We] hereby nominate [Property] as [my/our] main residence with effect from [Date]."

Unmarried Couples – Two Main Residences

While married couples enjoy a lot of tax benefits, unmarried couples are in a fortunate position when it comes to second homes.

This is because they can have two 'main residences', each qualifying for the principal private residence exemption. This means they can have two properties that are completely free from capital gains tax.

Example

Dean and Geri are unmarried and live together in Manchester in a house that they bought together as joint tenants. They also decide to buy a cottage in the Lake District.

Their accountant advises them to do as follows:

- Geri transfers her share of the Manchester house into Dean's sole name. There's no capital gains tax because this is her principal private residence.

- Geri buys the Lake District cottage in her sole name. This is now the only private residence she owns, so it should be regarded as her main residence and tax free.

- Each partner then makes a main residence election in favour of the property they own. This is an important precautionary measure because there is a slight chance the taxman might argue that each partner has an equitable stake in the other person's property. Making the elections puts the question of which property is which person's main residence beyond any doubt.

Establishing the Property as a Residence

The next thing Geri has to do is ensure that the second home does become her private residence.

Actual physical occupation of the property on a habitual basis is essential. Spending one weekend per month in the property, for example, should generally be sufficient.

This regular private use of the property would need to continue for a reasonable period. What is 'reasonable' depends on the facts of the case. Generally, we would recommend at least two years, although, where circumstances do genuinely prevent this, a shorter period might sometimes be acceptable.

More important than the amount of time is the 'quality' of the taxpayer's occupation of the property. This, for example, would include furnishing the property to a sufficient standard to make it a comfortable home.

It's also important not to advertise the property for sale or rent until the 'reasonable' period discussed above has expired.

Once the property ceases to be used by the owner as a private residence, it will cease to be treated as their main residence for capital gains tax purposes. Nevertheless, the principal private residence exemption will generally continue to cover the last three years of ownership of the property.

Renting Out Your Holiday Home

Generally speaking, the property cannot be regarded as a private residence when it is being used exclusively for some other purpose.

If you rent the property out under a formal lease, it will cease to be your private residence immediately. This is because the property will cease to be available to you as a private residence and the required 'habitual' occupation will no longer be possible.

Where the property is rented out for short periods, but not enough to prevent it from being regarded as the owner's home, then the principal private residence exemption may continue, but will be restricted by reference to the rental periods.

This brings us to the question of whether you can rent out your second home as holiday accommodation and still benefit from the principal private residence exemption.

Here we come back to the issue of your 'quality' of occupation. If the property is rented out to such an extent that your own enjoyment of the property is hindered to the point where it can no longer be regarded as a 'home', then you will lose the benefit of private residence status on the property from that point onwards.

It's worth remembering, however, that the tax advantages of a property which qualifies as 'furnished holiday accommodation' are significant. We'll take a closer look at furnished holiday lets shortly.

Furthermore, it is, in fact, conceivable for a property to qualify as both furnished holiday accommodation and as the owner's principal private residence at the same time, with some restriction to the principal private residence exemption.

Example

Bonnie and Clyde are unmarried and live together in a large house in Glasgow which is owned solely by Clyde.

In 2008, Bonnie buys a small cottage on Skye for £100,000. For the next twelve years she rents the cottage out as furnished holiday accommodation for 48 weeks each year. For the remaining four weeks each year, Bonnie occupies the cottage herself. Clyde sometimes joins her but sometimes has to remain in Glasgow on business.

Bonnie's regular occupation of her Skye cottage is enough to make it a residence. As Bonnie is the sole owner of the cottage and she and Clyde are unmarried, it makes no difference to the cottage's tax status whether he joins her in the cottage or not.

For the avoidance of doubt, Bonnie makes a main residence election in favour of her Skye cottage (within two years of buying it). Clyde should not need to make any election in respect of his

Glasgow home as, for him, there can be no doubt which property is his main residence.

In 2020, Bonnie sells the cottage, realising a total capital gain of £104,000.

As usual, Bonnie is entitled to full PPR relief for the last three years out of the twelve years she owned the property.

For the nine-year period from 2008 to 2017, Bonnie is only entitled to principal private residence relief on 4/52 of her capital gain, reflecting the 4 weeks per year she used the property privately.

Her total principal private residence relief therefore amounts to:

£104,000 x 9/12 x 4/52	£6,000
£104,000 x 3/12	£26,000
Total relief	£32,000

In addition, Bonnie will also be entitled to private letting relief of £32,000.

So even though she rented out the property most of the time, the fact that she has also used it as her main residence means she can exclude £64,000 of her profits from capital gains tax when she sells the property.

Tax Tip – Foreign Properties

A second home located abroad can be treated as one partner's main residence for capital gains tax purposes under exactly the same principles we already outlined.

Under the right circumstances, this provides scope to have a capital gains tax-free foreign holiday home!

Do watch out for foreign taxes though!

Wealth Warning

Where an unmarried couple hold property for their private use in a different proportion to the funds they provided, there is a risk of income tax charges under the 'pre-owned asset regime'.

These charges may also apply where one partner transfers a property, or a share of a property, to the other as a gift or sells it at below market value and continues to occupy it (as Geri did in our example above).

Such charges can easily be avoided by making an election to have the transferred property or donated funds included in the transferor's estate for inheritance tax purposes. There are some complex issues to be considered here however, so professional advice is needed as usual.

Something in the Garden

The last PPR issue we'd like to take a look at is how you can protect this valuable tax relief if you sell off or develop part of your home.

It's a common scenario: a taxpayer has a large garden so he or she sells part of it off for property development.

There are the right ways to do this and there are other ways, which are very, very wrong!

The Wrong Ways

For example, you should NOT:

- Sell your house first before selling the development plot.
- Fence off the development plot or separate it from the rest of your garden before selling it.
- Use the development plot for any purpose other than your own private residential occupation immediately prior to the sale.
- Allow the development plot to fall into disuse.

Each of these will result in the complete loss of your principal private residence exemption for the development plot. And, furthermore, do not assume that the plot is covered by the principal private residence exemption if the total area of your house and garden exceeds half a hectare.

The Right Ways

The easiest thing to do is simply sell off the land without committing any of the cardinal sins described above. This sale will now enjoy the same principal private residence exemption as applies to your house itself.

The Other 'Right Way'

The only drawback to the simple way is that you do not get to participate in any of the profit on the development of the plot.

But, what if you hang on to the plot and develop it yourself? You could then proceed to move into the new property and adopt it as your main residence which would be tax free.

Your old house can safely be sold at any time up to three years after the date you move out and still be covered by the principal private residence exemption.

The new house should be fully covered by the principal private residence exemption as long as you move in within a year of the date that development started.

There are some potential dangers here, but the exemption should be available if you genuinely adopt the new house as your new main residence.

If, however, the newly developed property were sold straight away, this would give rise to a trading profit which would be subject to income tax and national insurance.

Summary

So far we've looked at how capital gains tax is calculated, how you complete your tax return, and how you can make the most of the principal private residence tax break, including how you can make the most of the '3 year rule', how you can use elections to protect your holiday home from tax and how unmarried couples can have more than one principal residence.

Now we're going to take a look at a variety of other important capital gains tax planning issues.

This information should help you save extra tax and avoid making costly mistakes.

Chapter 8

Trading vs Investment

The first issue we should address is whether you are in fact subject to capital gains tax in the first place.

This revolves around whether you're a 'property trader' or 'property investor'.

Property trading includes activities like property refurbishment and development and property dealing.

If you're a property trader, you pay income tax on your property sales and if you're an investor you pay capital gains tax.

The following is a brief summary of the most important tax advantages and disadvantages of each type of property business.

Tax Advantages of Property Investment Businesses

- The best thing about being a property investor is you only pay 18% capital gains tax on profits from property sales.

- There are also a number of exemptions and reliefs you may be able to claim including:

    - The annual CGT exemption
    - Principal private residence relief, and
    - Private letting relief

Tax Disadvantages of Property Investment Businesses

However, being classified as a property investor also has a number of drawbacks. For example, there's very limited scope to offset your rental losses and capital losses.

Rental losses can only be offset against rental profits in future tax years but not against your other income, such as your salary.

Similarly, capital losses may only be offset against future capital gains.

Tax Advantages of Being a Property Trader

The advantages of being taxed as a property trader include:

- Losses can be set off against your other income.

- A property development business can be passed on to your heirs free from inheritance tax when you die.

- It's usually possible to move your business into a company or transfer it to family without any significant tax charges.

Tax Disadvantages of Property Trades

However, there are some serious drawbacks to being a property trader:

- Your profits are subject to both income tax and national insurance. This means you could end up paying up to 41% tax on your profits – 40% income tax and 1% national insurance.

- VAT registration may be compulsory if your annual turnover from certain trading activities exceeds £67,000.

Summary – Trading vs Investment

Most people would agree that being taxed as an investor is far more attractive than being taxed as a trader. Investors pay 18% tax at the very most – traders pay up to 41% tax.

However, you can't choose how you're taxed – it depends on how you act and your intentions.

Nevertheless, there are a couple of things we can say with reasonable certainty.

- If you buy a property and rent it out for several years you are a property investor and will pay capital gains tax when you sell. This is what you want because capital gains tax is usually much lower than income tax. The same goes for second home owners. If you buy a property and use it as a second home for several years you will pay capital gains tax.

- If you buy a property with the intention of doing it up and selling it immediately for a profit, you are a property trader and will have to pay income tax.

The Boundary Between Investment & Trading

In reality, however, some property investors' intentions are often not clear. If you ask someone what their plans are for their property investments you often hear answers like these:

> "I might sell it, or I might hang on to it for a while if I can't get a good price."

> "We think we'll rent it out for a few years, but we might sell if we get a good offer."

> "We'll probably sell a few and rent the rest out."

Naturally, any investor is going to do whatever produces the best result and if an unexpected opportunity comes along they would be foolish not to take it while they can.

For tax purposes though, what we have to do is to establish what the investor's main intention was, at the outset, when the investment was made.

The trouble with intentions, of course, is that they can be very difficult to prove. Who but you can possibly know exactly what was in your mind when you purchased a property?

Looking at it from the taxman's point of view, the only evidence which they sometimes have to go on are the actual facts of what really transpired and this may be very different to what was intended.

Tax Tip

For this reason, it is sensible to document your intentions for your property business.

This could take many forms. Some of the most popular are a business plan, a diary note, a letter to your solicitor, or a memo to a business partner.

Remember to date your documentary evidence.

Having something in writing will not necessarily be enough, however.

A business plan which says "we will rent the properties out for five years and then sell them" may not be very convincing if you actually sell all your properties very quickly.

Unless, that is, you sold them because of an unexpected change in circumstances.

Acceptable reasons for changing your mind could include:

- An unexpected shortage of funds
- An unexpected and exceptionally good offer
- Relocation due to work, family or other reasons
- Divorce or separation
- Bereavements and inheritance
- Concerns over the property market in a particular location
- Funds are required for an exceptional investment opportunity elsewhere

But Life Isn't Always That Simple

Between the extremes of the long-term investor and short-term trader is the 'grey area' where investment meets trading. It's not always so easy to be sure which side of the line you're on.

It is almost impossible for us to give you a definitive answer to explain exactly when investment becomes trading. Here, however, are some useful guidelines:

Renovation and Conversion Work

Renovation or building work may sometimes indicate that there is a trading motive behind buying the property.

However, if you continue to hold the property for several years after the completion of your building work, it is likely that you still have an investment property which will eventually be subject to capital gains tax.

On the other hand, if you sell the property immediately after completing the work, you may well be regarded as a property developer **unless** your original intention had been to keep the property and rent it out, but some change in circumstances led you to change your mind.

Frequency of Transactions

If you only sell a property once every few years, you are likely to be carrying on a property investment business.

If you make several sales every year, representing a high proportion of your portfolio, you may be a property trader or developer.

Number of Transactions

As well as their frequency, the number of property transactions which you have carried out can be a factor in deciding whether you are trading.

Many people like to buy a house, 'do it up', then sell it and move on. If you do this once then you're probably nothing other than a normal homeowner in the eyes of Revenue & Customs. If you do it every six months for ten years, then somewhere along the way you have probably become a property developer.

Finance Arrangements

Long-term finance arrangements, such as mortgages are generally indicative of an investment activity.

Financing your business through short-term arrangements, such as bank overdrafts will be more indicative of a development or dealing trade. Short-term finance tends to indicate short-term assets.

Length of Ownership

There is no definitive rule as to how long you must hold a property for it to be an investment rather than potentially trading stock.

Naturally, however, the longer the period that you generally hold your properties, the more likely they are to be accepted as investment properties.

Renting the Properties Out

Renting properties out is usually definitive proof that they are being held as investments and not part of a property trade. Like everything else on this list though, it may not be conclusive on its own.

Living in a Property

Living in the property is another useful way to help prove that your intention was to hold it as a long-term asset. Once again though, this may not be enough if the other facts of the case prove to be contrary to this idea.

'Hands On' Involvement

Being actively involved in the renovation or development of a property makes you look like a property developer. Contracting all of the work out looks more like property investment.

Wealth Warning

Remember that everything we have discussed in this section is merely one factor in determining what kind of property business you have.

Ultimately, it is the overall picture formed by your intentions, your behaviour and your investment pattern which will eventually decide whether you have a property investment business or a property trade.

Mixed Property Businesses

What if your business doesn't fit neatly into investment or trading?

If you have a 'mixed' property business, involving both investment and trading, there is a great danger that any property development or property trading may effectively 'taint' what would otherwise be a property investment business. The taxman may then attempt to deny you capital gains tax treatment on all of your property transactions.

Tax Tip

To avoid this danger, you should take whatever steps you can to separate the businesses.

For example, you could:

- Draw up separate accounts for each business.
- Use a different business name for each activity.
- Report the non-investment activities as a different business in your tax return.
- Consider a different legal ownership structure for the non-investment activities (for example, put them in a company or a partnership with your spouse, partner or adult children).

Chapter 9

How to Structure Your Property Investments

Joint Ownership

If you are taxed as an investor, rather than a trader, and therefore subject to capital gains tax one of the things you'll want to get right is the ownership structure of your properties.

In this section we'll look at the tax benefits of joint ownership. If you own a property jointly with someone else you can either end up paying more capital gains tax or less. Let's have a quick look at the tax benefits of joint ownership first.

Tax Benefits of Joint Ownership

With joint ownership the potential capital gains tax saving on a regular buy-to-let property is £1,728.

Why? Because having one more owner, such as your spouse or partner, means another CGT exemption can be used when you sell. This means an extra £9,600 of gains will be tax free:

£9,600 x 18% tax = £1,728

If the property has been your main home in the past, your spouse or partner may also qualify for additional private letting relief of up to £40,000. This means another £40,000 of gains could be tax free, saving you up to £7,200 in capital gains tax.

£40,000 x 18% tax = £7,200

Tax Drawbacks of Joint Ownership

It usually pays to own property jointly but there are circumstances where this may not produce any tax savings, for example where:

- One of you has already used up your CGT exemption for the year by selling another property or asset.

- One of you has capital losses to use up. For example, if you have £20,000 of capital losses from selling some shares, you can offset these against the property gain. In this situation you may save more tax if you own all of the property.

Getting the Ownership Structure Right

Here are some important planning points if you decide to change the ownership of the property before you sell it to save tax:

- Do the transfer as soon as possible, ideally before the property is put on the market.
- Transfers after there's a sale contract will probably be ineffective.
- The person who receives a share of the property must have proper beneficial ownership. Otherwise the transfer will be invalid for tax purposes.
- Joint ownership does not have to mean equal shares – any allocation is possible.
- Married couples can transfer shares of a property to each other without any capital gains tax consequences.
- Unmarried couples aren't so lucky. Such transfers are treated as if the property share had been sold for its open market value. This could result in a significant CGT bill.
- There are ways to avoid this, for example by making a transfer of property into a trust. This allows you to postpone paying capital gains tax. However, such an arrangement costs money and may not be worthwhile if the capital gains tax savings are small.
- Finally, ask yourself are the tax savings worth it? The maximum CGT saving for transferring a regular buy to let property that you've never lived in is just £1,728. From that you'll also have to deduct legal fees and any other costs.

Saving Other Taxes

The biggest tax savings you'll get from joint ownership are income tax not capital gains tax savings.

In the best case scenario you could save around £9,000 in income tax if you're a 40% taxpayer and the other owner pays income tax at just 20% or perhaps even 0%.

However, for joint ownership to produce income tax savings two things are necessary:

- You have to own properties that actually produce rental profits – many buy-to let investors make rental losses.

- One of you must be paying income tax at 20% or less. This means one of you has to be earning less than around £41,000 per year.

Helping Your Children

It's not just your spouse or partner who can help you save tax – children can come in jolly useful too!

Each unmarried adult is entitled to have their own main private residence which is exempt from capital gains tax.

Once your children reach the age of 18 therefore, it is possible to put some tax-free capital growth into their hands.

The method is fairly straightforward: all that you need to do is purchase a property in their name which they then move into and adopt as their main residence.

Financing can be achieved in a number of ways, but the important point is that the adult child must have legal and beneficial title to the property.

So this technique should only be undertaken if you are prepared to pass wealth on to the children.

The purchase of the property has possible inheritance tax implications but these are avoided simply by surviving for seven years.

One final word of warning, though. You should be careful not to make any use of the property yourself since, if you have provided the funds for its purchase, any subsequent occupation by you or your spouse may give rise to an income tax charge under the 'pre-owned assets' regime.

Setting Up Your Own Property Company

No discussion of the ownership structure of your properties would be complete without taking a look at the pros and cons of setting up your very own property company.

This is a complex subject and, in fact, Taxcafe has devoted a whole publication to it called *Using a Property Company to Save Tax*.

However, it's important to remember that if you decide to transfer your existing property portfolio into a company this will be treated as a disposal and you will have to pay capital gains tax.

That's why it's often better to make **new** property purchases through a company, rather than transfer your existing properties.

So what's the best way to invest in property now – individually or using a company?

The new 18% capital gains tax rate only applies to private individuals who sell properties.

Companies don't pay capital gains tax – they pay corporation tax – and are completely unaffected by the new CGT rules.

In the near future, the corporation tax rate for small companies will be increased to 22%. On the face of it corporation tax of 22% is worse than capital gains tax at 18%.

Furthermore, companies do not get an annual capital gains tax exemption which means they cannot protect up to £9,600 of profits from tax, as private individuals can.

However, companies do offer a number of tax benefits.

For starters they qualify for indexation relief which protects them from inflation. Individuals do not.

Indexation relief is very valuable. If a property goes up by 5% per year over the next 15 years, a private individual could pay capital gains tax on the full 5%. But a company will only pay tax on part of that growth. For example, if inflation averages 3%, the company will only be taxed on 2%:

5% growth – 3% inflation = 2% taxable.

This is actually a simplistic example of how indexation relief works but it proves the point.

Another big tax benefit of using a company to invest in property is that companies can potentially offset their rental losses against their taxable gains.

Why is this valuable? Most investors who have borrowed money in recent years to buy investment property are sitting on rental losses. In other words, the rents are not big enough to cover the mortgages and all the other costs. This can go on for years and years, as any experienced investor will testify.

If you're an individual investor, the problem with these losses is you can't do much with them. They cannot be offset against your salary or other non-property income and they can't be used to reduce your capital gains tax when you sell a property.

All you can do is wait until your properties start making taxable rental profits, at which point your accumulated rental losses can be used to save income tax. This could be many years into the future. In fact it might never happen.

Many investors waste these accumulated rental losses because they sell their properties before they produce any rental profits.

Companies are in a much more favourable position when it comes to using their accumulated rental losses. A company can offset its rental losses against its capital gains from selling property.

For example, let's say your company sells a property and makes a gain of £20,000. If the company has accumulated £20,000 of rental losses over the years it won't pay a penny in tax on that capital gain.

Finally, remember that tax is just one factor to consider and there are lots of non-tax reasons for using a company.

For example, they're ideal when you want to share ownership with other people such as friends and family and also provide an element of legal protection because they are separate legal entities.

Summary

- Individuals pay 18% tax on their capital gains

- Companies pay 22% tax – possibly more

- Individuals enjoy an annual CGT exemption

- ... but companies get indexation relief

- ... and can offset their rental losses against their capital gains

- ... and there are other non-tax reasons why companies are attractive.

Chapter 10

Tax Benefits & Dangers of Remortgaging

Getting the ownership structure for your properties right is imperative and involving your spouse and children, or setting up your own property company, could potentially save you thousands of pounds in tax.

Another thing you have to structure carefully are your borrowings. A lot of property investors re-mortgage their properties. This is one way of getting your hands on your profits without having to sell any of your properties.

The good news is this money is completely tax free.

For example, let's say your property increases in value by £25,000 and you are able to borrow an extra £20,000 by remortgaging.

That money can be used as a deposit on another buy-to-let property or you could use it to pay for personal living expenses, children's education, a new car, or a holiday even.

Either way, the whole £20,000 is yours and you don't have to pay any tax on it.

Capital gains tax generally only comes into the picture when there is a property disposal. If you re-mortgage a property you haven't made a disposal because you still own it. So there's no capital gains tax to pay.

Remortgaging is a good way of avoiding tax initially but there are some long-term dangers you have to be aware of.

But first of all let's look briefly at the income tax consequences.

Income Tax

When you remortgage you will, of course, have to pay interest.

The question is whether that interest is tax deductible.

In most cases, it doesn't matter whether you remortgage your own home or a buy-to-let property. Whether the interest is tax deductible generally depends on one thing and one thing alone – how you **use** the money.

Use it to buy a new investment property and the interest is tax deductible.

If you use the money for personal reasons – to pay for a new car, for example – the interest is not generally tax deductible.

There is an important exception to this rule, however. When you re-mortgage a rental property up to the level of that property's value when it was first introduced into your rental business, your mortgage interest is **always** tax deductible; whatever you spend the money on!

Dangers of Remortgaging

A lot of property investors forget that remortgaging does not reduce your capital gains tax bill, it simply postpones it.

If and when you eventually sell the property you will have to pay the bank back all the money you borrowed and you will have to pay the taxman all your capital gains tax.

Remember that when you calculate your capital gains tax you cannot deduct the mortgage over the property. Mortgages have absolutely nothing to do with capital gains tax. They cannot be claimed as an expense.

Where you have to be very careful is if property prices fall. We know falling property prices is something none of us likes to talk about but, if you remortgage your properties too aggressively, you may not have enough money at the end of the day to pay back your loans and pay your capital gains tax.

Example

Steve bought a property for £200,000. Over the years it increased in value to £450,000 and Steve remortgaged up to 85% which is £382,500.

Now let's say there's a downturn in the property market and his property falls in value by 10% so it's now worth £405,000.

He then decides to sell. He receives £405,000 from the sale but how much is left over for Steve after repaying the bank and the taxman?

If we assume he has buying and selling costs of £3,000 each, his capital gains tax calculation looks like this.

Sales proceeds	£405,000
Less: Purchase price	£200,000
Less: Selling costs	£3,000
Less: Purchase costs	£3,000
Less: CGT exemption	£9,600
Chargeable gain	£189,400
Tax @ 18%	£34,092

He also has to pay back the bank £382,500, so overall Steve is left with a shortfall of £14,592, calculated as follows:

£405,000 - £3,000 selling costs - £382,500 mortgages - £34,092 tax
= -£14,592

That money will have to come from somewhere else because there isn't enough money from the property sale to cover all the loans and tax.

Escaping the Trap

Steve's story may be a worst case scenario but we've met lots of property investors who could easily end up in a very similar position.

To avoid this trap investors have to borrow responsibly, taking account of their future CGT bills.

In theory, with a capital gains tax rate of just 18%, you should never borrow more than the cost of the property plus 82% of any increase in value:

Maximum borrowing = Original cost + 82% profits

However, this could still leave you vulnerable to a downturn in property values.

So we would tend to suggest reducing this figure by at least another 10% to safeguard against any nasty surprises.

Interest vs Capital Gains Tax

Although mortgage brokers and banks love it when you remortgage your properties, we're not convinced it's always the best thing to do, especially now that the maximum capital gains tax rate has fallen so dramatically.

It's a good idea when the property market is strong and you want to use the money to buy more investment properties.

But when the property market is slowing down or interest rates are high it may be more sensible to keep your borrowings down and reduce the risk in your buy-to-let portfolio.

We're also not convinced that remortgaging is a good idea if you take the money and spend it on personal items such as general living expenses. In these cases, the interest isn't tax deductible and will soon add up.

For example, let's say you own a property which has increased in value by £30,000. If you sell it your capital gains tax bill could be £1,944, if you own it jointly with a spouse or partner.

Let's say instead you remortgage the property and borrow that £30,000. If your interest rate is, say, 6.5%, your annual interest cost will be more than your tax bill from selling the property:

£30,000 x 6.5% = £1,950

The difference is that interest has to be paid, not just once like capital gains tax, but every year!

So remortgaging can postpone tax in the short run but it can also be extremely expensive in other ways.

Are we saying that you should sell your properties instead of remortgaging them? Not necessarily. You may have good reasons to hold onto your properties for many years into the future.

However, you should always think twice about remortgaging a property just to get your hands on some cash to spend.

Chapter 11

Improvements vs Repairs

You can't deduct your mortgages when you calculate CGT but one big cost you can deduct is improvements.

However, a lot of investors don't fully understand the tax difference between repairs and improvements.

Repairs are an income tax deduction and can be claimed every year when you do your tax return.

Improvements can only be claimed when you sell your property and calculate your capital gains tax.

The question is: what is a repair and what is an improvement?

It's a crucial question because repairs can give you immediate tax relief at rates of up to 40p in the £1, whereas improvements can only be claimed when you sell your property and only save you tax at the rate of 18p in the £1.

On the other hand, if you already have enough surplus rental losses to cover your rental profits for years to come, getting relief for improvements is sometimes more valuable.

We'll try to provide some answers to the repairs versus improvements question in the pages that follow. However, it's important to stress that deciding what is a repair and what is an improvement can be a complex issue and it is essential to consult a tax professional if significant amounts of money are involved.

Freestanding Items

First of all, it's important to realise that only fitted items that are part of the fabric of your property, such as new windows, fitted kitchens and bathrooms, can be classed as improvements and deducted when you calculate your capital gains tax.

When it comes to freestanding items such as carpets, curtains, electrical goods and appliances, these items can never be claimed as improvements.

For a detailed discussion of the income tax treatment of these items, we would recommend picking up a copy of Taxcafe's guide *How to Avoid Property Tax*.

Back to Repairs vs Improvements

So what are repairs and improvements? There are two basic principles:

- Spending which **restores** the property to its previous condition is a repair.

- Spending which **enhances** the condition of the property beyond what it used to be is an improvement.

Example 1

Geri has a small townhouse in Kensington which she rents out. She decides to build a conservatory costing £40,000, including £2,000 to redecorate the adjoining room.

Geri's conservatory is an improvement because she is enhancing the condition of the property. So she can only claim the expense when she sells the property and does her CGT calculation.

Redecorating is usually allowed as a repair but in this case it's part of the overall capital expenditure because it's a necessary part of the building work.

Example 2

Emma owns a row of shops which she has been renting out. A massive storm damages the roofs and Emma has these repaired at a cost of £50,000. Emma's cost is a repair cost which she can claim against her rental income.

It's a repair because she is restoring her property to its previous condition.

Emma Example Continued

The same storm also damaged several windows in Emma's shops. The glazier advises that it will be cheaper to replace the original wooden frames with new PVC double glazing and she agrees to do this. This expenditure is a repair, despite the fact that the new windows represent an improvement on the old ones.

This is because if, due to changes in fashion, or technological advances, it becomes cheaper or more efficient to replace something with a more modern alternative, the fact it's an improvement can be ignored and the expense can be classed as a repair.

Example 3

Victoria has a flat which she has been renting to students. She decides to upgrade it for the young professional market. Her costs are as follows:

- £16,000 on a new fitted kitchen.

- £3,500 redecorating the bathroom, including £2,000 to replace the existing toilet, sink and bath and £500 to install a shower (there was only a bath before).

- £3,000 repainting the rest of the flat.

- £3,000 on rewiring.

How much is repairs and how much is improvements? Remember the repairs can be claimed as a tax deduction when she fills in her annual tax return. The improvements can be deducted when she sells the property and does her CGT calculation.

The Kitchen

The cost of a new fitted kitchen replacing a broadly similar one would be a repair expense. This would extend to the costs of re-tiling, re-plastering, plumbing, etc.

If Victoria's new kitchen has extra storage or other extra features which weren't present before, then a proportion of the expense will be treated as a capital improvement.

In an extreme case, where fairly standard units are replaced by expensive customised items using much higher quality materials, then the whole cost of the new kitchen will need to be regarded as a capital improvement.

Bathroom

Replacing the existing toilet, basin and sink should usually be a tax deductible repair.

Once again replacing these existing fittings with expensive customised ones would amount to a capital improvement.

Fitting the new shower will definitely be a capital improvement as this is an item of equipment which was not present before.

The remaining bathroom redecoration costs will need to be apportioned between repairs and improvements. Any expense arising due to the installation of the new shower will be treated as an improvement.

Redecorating the Flat

Most of the redecoration work, in the absence of any building work in the rooms concerned, should be fairly straightforward repairs expenditure.

Rewiring

The rewiring cost will be fully tax deductible as a repair if it is simply 'new for old'. If, on the other hand, Victoria took the opportunity to fit a few new sockets then there will be an improvement element and, as usual, an apportionment would be required.

Newly Acquired Properties

We've already stated that spending which restores the property to its previous condition is a repair.

However, it's important to point out that when we talk about 'previous condition' we're talking about since **you** have owned the property – not before.

So if you buy a property with a hole in the roof, the cost of repairing the roof will be a capital improvement.

Where both building work and redecoration take place simultaneously in a newly acquired property, it is likely that all of the expenditure will be regarded as a capital improvement.

However, simply modernising the décor in a newly acquired property, when no other work is undertaken, would generally continue to be a repair expense.

The Taxman's View on Newly Acquired Properties

In the case of any expenditure on newly acquired rental properties, Revenue & Customs' own manuals specifically state that any expenditure which is not allowed for income tax purposes on the grounds that it represents capital expenditure should then be allowed for capital gains tax purposes on a disposal of that same property.

Chapter 12

Making the Most of Your Annual CGT Exemption

Claiming all your improvement costs can reduce your capital gains tax bill significantly.

The other big deduction you can claim, of course, is the annual CGT exemption. This can reduce your taxable profits by up to £9,600 per year if you're single and £19,200 in the case of couples.

This can save you a lot of tax if you sell your property portfolio over a number of years and therefore make use of not just one but lots of annual exemptions.

It's one of the simplest capital gains tax saving strategies around!

Example

Let's say Paul and Carrie have achieved their dream of becoming property millionaires. They've built up a portfolio of 20 properties with total net profits of £1 million.

They now want to start selling them to reap the rewards of their hard work.

I'm not going to make any assumptions about their ages or their other income or wealth. But I am going to assume that they don't need to sell all the properties immediately. They're happy to sell them off at the rate of one per year. Each property has made a profit of £50,000 and receiving a lump sum of this amount every year is enough to make a significant difference to their lifestyle.

To keep things really simple I'm keeping everything fixed in the years ahead – the value of their properties, tax rates and allowances etc.

So how much capital gains tax will they pay? Every time they sell a property they have to pay £5,544 in capital gains tax:

This is calculated as follows:

Net Profit	£50,000
Less: 2 Annual CGT exemptions	£19,200
Chargeable gain	£30,800
Tax @ 18%	£5,544

Their effective tax rate is only 11%, compared with the maximum capital gains tax rate of 18% or the maximum income tax rate of 40%. If this was salary income, the tax could be around £20,000.

By selling only one of their 20 properties each year they save £65,664 in capital gains tax. Why? Because they get to use their combined annual CGT exemption (£19,200) an extra 19 times:

$$19 \times £19,200 \times 18\% \text{ tax} = £65,664$$

Let's say they want to speed things up a bit and sell two properties per year. In that case they'll realise profits of £100,000 every year and get to use their combined annual CGT exemption an extra 9 times, saving them an extra £31,104 in capital gains tax.

$$9 \times £19,200 \times 18\% = £31,104$$

The point I'm trying to make is that you don't have to resort to complex and expensive tax planning to slash your CGT bill. One of the simplest strategies is to spread your sales over several years to make the most of your annual CGT exemptions.

Small Properties vs Big Properties

For similar reasons it also pays, purely from a tax standpoint, to have lots of small properties rather than one or two big ones.

You can do this either by:

- Buying lower value properties, or
- Investing in syndicates or jointly with other people.

This will allow you to eventually spread your sales over a number of tax years and make maximum use of your annual CGT exemption.

From a non tax standpoint this is not necessarily the best strategy, however.

The more properties you have the more time consuming it is to manage your portfolio.

Furthermore, the more properties you buy and sell the more costs you will incur (legal fees, etc).

At Taxcafe we always say that you should never let the tax tail wag the investment dog.

In other words, tax should only be one factor you consider when you decide whether a property is worth buying.

Nevertheless, it is interesting to note that a couple with £60,000 in profits spread over three properties can sell one per tax year and pay just a few hundred pounds in CGT.

However, a couple with £60,000 of profits tied up in just one property could end up paying over £7,000 in tax when they sell because they will only be able to use one year's worth of CGT exemptions.

Protecting Your Rental Losses

In the example we just looked at Paul and Carrie sold their properties over a number of years to save capital gains tax. Another reason it pays to sell your properties gradually is to save income tax.

Most property investors make a rental loss thanks to their mortgage interest and all their other costs such as letting agent fees, wear and tear, and repairs.

Over many years these losses could run to tens of thousands of pounds, especially if you have a big portfolio.

Unfortunately rental losses cannot be offset against your salary or other income to reduce your tax bill. The taxman does, however, let you save up your losses each year and use them to reduce tax when your properties eventually start producing rental profits.

Every £1,000 of rental loss is worth up to £400 in income tax savings, so they're extremely valuable.

However – and this is the important bit – if you sell ALL your rental properties these valuable rental losses are wiped out.

Rental losses can only be carried forward as long as you continue to have a property rental business.

If you're selling UK properties the trick is to keep at least one UK rental property – that way you will still have a UK property business and your losses can be preserved.

Example

Let's say that like Paul and Carrie you own 20 valuable properties which you decide to sell. Let's also say you've accumulated £100,000 worth of rental losses over many years. We've pulled this figure out of the hat. In practice the number could be bigger or smaller depending on how big your mortgages are and how much rent the properties have generated over the years.

If you sell all of your properties in one go your property business will cease to exist and your losses will be lost forever.

If, however, you sell your properties over a number of years you can use the proceeds to reduce the borrowings on the properties you still own.

As your mortgages go down your properties will start making bigger and bigger rental profits. Rental profits are taxable but because you have accumulated losses of £100,000 you can earn £100,000 of rental income tax free. As a result you could save up to £40,000 in income tax:

£100,000 x 40% = £40,000 tax saving

Chapter 13

Emigrating to Avoid Capital Gains Tax

The Paul and Carrie example showed how easy it is to reduce your effective CGT rate from 18% to about 11%.

But what if you want to completely avoid capital gains tax altogether?

Probably the most drastic thing you can do in that case is leave the country.

A few years ago it was possible to go and live in certain countries for just one year and completely avoid paying tax on your investment profits.

This was a fantastic loophole, especially when capital gains tax was up to 40%.

Since then, two things have happened:

- First of all you now have to live abroad for at least five complete tax years – that's a long time to live away from your friends and family.

- The second thing that's happened is the maximum capital gains tax rate has fallen from 40% to 18%. Many people will now feel less desire to move overseas purely to avoid tax.

For example, let's say you have a portfolio with £250,000 of profits. The maximum tax you will pay is £45,000:

£250,000 x 18% = £45,000

Would you be willing to live overseas for five years to save £45,000 in tax? That's a tax saving of just £9,000 per year. Some people would, but most probably wouldn't. Remember, moving abroad is an expensive and time consuming business and these costs will eat into your tax savings.

What if you have £1 million of profits? In that case, the maximum tax you will pay is £180,000:

$$£1 \text{ million} \times 18\% = £180,000$$

Would you be willing to live overseas for five years to save £180,000 in tax? That's a tax saving of £36,000 per year. Many people would be willing to and others wouldn't.

Of course, if you plan to emigrate one day anyway, this is all academic. You may be able to live in the country of your dreams **and** avoid paying tax at the same time.

However, you have to make sure you sell your UK assets in the right way because there are significant traps awaiting the unwary.

It is necessary to become non-UK ordinarily resident, as well as non-UK resident.

This is a complex field of tax planning, however the key points worth noting are:

- Emigration must generally be permanent, or at least long-term (usually at least five complete UK tax years).

- You must not sell any assets until non-residence has been achieved.

- Your property sales must be delayed until the tax year <u>after</u> the year you emigrate.

- Limited return visits to the UK are permitted.

- If you return permanently to the UK before 5 years are up you will have to pay all the capital gains tax.

- Finally, it's essential to make sure you do not end up paying capital gains tax in another country – there's no point in 'jumping out of the frying pan and into the fire!'

Return Visits

As we said limited return visits to the UK are permitted. The general rules on return visits are:

- They must not exceed 182 days in any one UK tax year.

- They must average less than 91 days per year.

From 2008/9 onwards, days of arrival and departure in and out of the UK are counted as part of the visit for these purposes.

However, it's important to stress that this is only one factor which determines your non-resident status.

In practice, Revenue and Customs will look at many other factors and the more links you maintain with the UK the more likely you are to continue to be UK resident and liable for capital gains tax.

Chapter 14

Enterprise Investment Schemes

If you don't want to emigrate and don't want to pay any capital gains tax when you sell your properties one solution is to reinvest your proceeds in Enterprise Investment Scheme shares.

These investments let you postpone capital gains tax and help you reduce your income tax.

The investment must take place within three years of selling the property. It can also take place up to a year before you sell the property.

It is even possible to defer capital gains tax by investing in your own trading company!

Unfortunately, however, companies involved in property are generally ineligible to issue Enterprise Investment Scheme shares.

Alternatively, there are products which let you spread your risk when investing in these intrinsically risky investments.

There's no limit on the amount which can be invested in Enterprise Investment Scheme shares if you need to defer a big capital gain.

However, it's important to stress that Enterprise Investment Schemes let you **postpone** capital gains tax but do not avoid it altogether. The gain you postpone becomes subject to capital gains tax when those shares are sold.

From 6th April 2008, qualifying investments of up to £500,000 per year in an unconnected company may also carry an income tax credit of up to 20% of the amount invested.

In other words, if you invest £100,000 you will reduce your income tax on your salary or other income by £20,000.

Combining the Income Tax credit with the Capital Gains Tax deferral makes these investments extremely powerful tax shelters.

Chapter 15

Furnished Holiday Lettings

Another way of deferring capital gains tax is to invest in furnished holiday lets.

These are almost the only type of property investment which allow an investor to sell one property and postpone capital gains tax by investing in another. This lets you sell properties in areas that are underperforming and seek out new properties in up and coming 'hotspots', without fear of losing a big chunk of your profits to the taxman.

Note, however, that you cannot defer capital gains tax on a regular buy-to-let property by reinvesting in a furnished holiday let. You can only defer tax by selling either a furnished holiday let or your own business trading premises and buying either another holiday let or new trading premises.

Furnished holiday lets offer lots of other tax benefits as well. Getting one of your properties to qualify is the property tax equivalent of winning the lottery!

The other tax benefits include:

- Holdover relief for gifts – this lets you give your property to your family and postpone the payment of capital gains tax.

- Entrepreneurs Relief – This new relief was introduced on 6th April 2008. When you sell furnished holiday lets you can have up to £1 million of gains taxed at just 10%. The £1 million is a lifetime limit but each individual qualifies, so couples can have up to £2 million worth of gains taxed at just 10%.

- Losses may be set off against your other income, such as your salary.

- A furnished holiday letting business may also be exempt from inheritance tax.

The letting of holiday accommodation is, however, standard-rated for VAT. You therefore have to register for VAT if annual income from holiday lets exceeds the VAT registration threshold, currently £67,000.

Qualification

So how do you qualify for all these tax breaks? The property must be:

- Situated in the UK

- Fully furnished

- Available for letting to holidaymakers for at least 140 days a year (these must be proper commercial lets, not discounted rates for your mates!)

- Actually let for at least 70 days (commercial lets only again)

- Not occupied for more than 31 days by the same person in any 7 month period.

Whilst the property need not be in a recognised holiday area, the lettings should strictly be to holidaymakers and tourists in order to qualify.

The added cherry on top is that there is nothing to stop you from using the property occasionally, although this will reduce the income tax and capital gains tax reliefs you can claim.

However, whether you use the property or not, you must ensure that, taken as a whole, the property remains a commercially viable, i.e. profitable, proposition in the long run.

Chapter 16

Entrepreneurs Relief

We mentioned that UK furnished holiday lets qualify for the new Entrepreneurs Relief that was introduced on 6th April 2008.

This allows up to £1 million worth of gains be taxed at just 10% instead of 18%.

The only other type of property that qualifies for this relief would be the trading premises of your business.

Lots of businessmen and women own their own business premises personally. One of the tax reliefs these properties used to qualify for was business asset taper relief. This was a fantastic tax relief that sheltered up to three quarters of your profits from the taxman, resulting in an effective capital gains tax rate of just 10%.

In fact this relief was available not just for your business premises but other commercial property investments as well.

Taper relief has now been abolished and most commercial property investments are taxed in exactly the same way as residential properties.

The new Entrepreneurs Relief is, however, useful to business owners who sell their trading premises, although there are some tough restrictions:

- Firstly, your property generally only qualifies if you're also selling the business.

- Secondly, the relief is only available if your business carries on a 'qualifying trade'. As usual, property investment does not qualify, although property development might.

- Lastly, the property only qualifies for the maximum relief if there was no rent payment from the business to you.

The last point is the real killer blow and will prevent many company owners and business partners from claiming this relief.

Most people who own their own premises get their companies or business partnerships to pay them rent.

If the rent you receive is the full market rent for the property then you will not be able to claim any Entrepreneurs Relief when you sell the property.

However, if you pay a lower than market rent then you can claim a proportionately lower amount of Entrepreneurs Relief.

Chapter 17

Capital Gains Tax vs Inheritance Tax

That brings us pretty much to the end. We'd like to finish up with just a few words about inheritance tax, which seems fitting since it's the last tax you'll ever pay!

One of the worst things about taxes is that they often interact with each other. You may do something to avoid one tax and end up paying more of another.

This is certainly the case with two of the UK's most hated taxes: capital gains tax and inheritance tax.

For detailed information on inheritance tax we would recommend the Taxcafe guide *How to Avoid Inheritance Tax*. Having said that, the basic rules can be summarised as follows:

- If you give someone a property, make sure you don't use it or benefit from it. If you then survive for seven years you won't have to pay any inheritance tax on that property.

- You may still have to pay capital gains tax, however.

- The taxman will generally treat the gift as a sale at full market value. So you will avoid inheritance tax but have to pay capital gains tax on your profits.

- One way to get around this is to gift assets which will not result in a capital gains tax charge, including cash or newly acquired assets which haven't risen in value much.

- Gifts to your spouse are usually exempt from both capital gains tax and inheritance tax.

- In other cases, another possible method is to use a trust. Using a trust, it is sometimes possible to transfer property to an unmarried partner, an adult child or another person free from both capital gains tax and inheritance tax. This is complex tax planning so professional advice is essential.

Thanks

Finally, we would like to thank you for reading this guide and we hope you found it useful.

Good luck with your property investments!

TAX Cafe®

Pay Less Tax!

...with help from Taxcafe's unique tax guides and software

All products available online at **www.taxcafe.co.uk/books**

How to Avoid Property Tax
By Carl Bayley BSc ACA

How to Avoid Property Tax is widely regarded as *the* tax bible for property investors. This unique and bestselling guide is jam packed with ideas that will save you thousands in income tax and capital gains tax.

"A valuable guide to the tax issues facing buy-to-let investors" - THE INDEPENDENT

How to Avoid Tax on Foreign Property
By Carl Bayley BSc ACA

Find out everything you need to know about paying less tax on overseas property. Completely up to date with key UK and overseas tax changes.

Using a Property Company to Save Tax
By Carl Bayley

Currently a 'hot topic' for the serious property investor, this guide shows how you can significantly boost your after-tax returns by setting up your own property company and explains ALL the tax consequences of property company ownership.

"An excellent tax resource....informative and clearly written" **The Letting Update Journal**

Keeping It Simple
By James Smith BSc ACA

This plain-English guide tells you everything you need to know about small business bookkeeping, accounting, tax returns and VAT.

Property Capital Gains Tax Calculator
By Carl Bayley

This powerful piece of software will calculate in seconds the capital gains tax payable when you sell a property and help you cut the tax bill. It provides tax planning tips based on your personal circumstances and a concise summary and detailed breakdown of all calculations.

Non-Resident & Offshore Tax Planning
By Lee Hadnum LLB ACA CTA

By becoming non-resident or moving your assets offshore it is possible to cut your tax bill to zero. This guide explains what you have to do and all the traps to avoid. Also contains detailed info on using offshore trusts and companies.

"The ultimate guide to legal tax avoidance" **Shelter Offshore**

The World's Best Tax Havens
By Lee Hadnum

This book provides a fascinating insight into the glamorous world of tax havens and how you can use them to cut your taxes to zero and safeguard your financial freedom.

How to Avoid Inheritance Tax
By Carl Bayley

Making sure you adequately plan for inheritance tax could save you literally hundreds of thousands of pounds. *How to Avoid Inheritance Tax* is a unique guide which will tell you all you need to know about sheltering your family's money from the taxman. This guide is essential reading for parents, grandparents and adult children.

"Useful source of Inheritance Tax information" **What Investment Magazine**

Using a Company to Save Tax
By Lee Hadnum

By running your business through a limited company you stand to save tens of thousands of pounds in tax and national insurance every year. This tax guide tells you everything you need to know about the tax benefits of incorporation.

Salary versus Dividends
By Carl Bayley

This unique guide is essential reading for anyone running their business as a limited company. After reading it, you will know the most tax efficient way in which to extract funds from your company, and save thousands in tax!

Selling Your Business
By Lee Hadnum

This guide tells you everything you need to know about paying less tax and maximizing your profits when you sell your business. It is essential reading for anyone selling a company or sole trader business.

How to Avoid Tax on Stock Market Profits
By Lee Hadnum

This tax guide can only be described as THE definitive tax-saving resource for stock market investors and traders. Anyone who owns shares, unit trusts, ISAs, corporate bonds or other financial assets should read it as it contains a huge amount of unique tax planning information.

Tax-Free Property Investments
By Nick Braun PhD

This guide shows you how to double your investment returns using a variety of powerful tax shelters. You'll discover how to buy property at a 40% discount, paid for by the taxman, never pay tax on your property profits again and invest tax free in overseas property.

How to Build a £4 Million Property Portfolio: Lifetime Lessons of a Student Landlord
By Tony Bayliss

Tony Bayliss is one of the UK's most successful student property investors. In *How to Build a £4 Million Property Portfolio* he reveals all his secrets – how he picks the best and most profitable student properties; how he markets his properties and how he enjoys capital growth of 12% pa, year in year out.

Printed in the United Kingdom
by Lightning Source UK Ltd.
129082UK00001B/151-198/P